Disability PRIDE

Inclusion Matters

Michelle Denton

PowerKiDS press

Published in 2025 by The Rosen Publishing Group, Inc.
2544 Clinton Street, Buffalo, NY 14224

Editor: Michele Suchomel-Casey
Book Design: Leslie Taylor

Photo Credits: Cover KOTOIMAGES/Shutterstock.com; (series background) P.siripak/Shutterstock.com, (series disability pride colors) rudall30/Shutterstock.com; p. 5 PeopleImages.com - Yuri A/Shutterstock.com, (flag sidebar) Maxim Studio/Shutterstock.com; p. 7 Harris & Ewing/LOC.com; (inset at top) Internet Archive Book Images/Wiki Commons_File:Care and education of crippled children in the United States (1914) (14800473853).jpg; p. 9 Jaguar PS/Shutterstock.com; p. 11 wavebreakmedia/Shutterstock.com; p. 13 ABO PHOTOGRAPHY/Shutterstock.com; p. 15 Eugene Powers/Shutterstock.com; p. 17 Rawpixel.com/Shutterstock.com; p. 19 Gorodenkoff/Shutterstock.com; p. 21 Rawpixel.com/Shutterstock.com, (inset) Logan Bush/Shutterstock.com.

Cataloging-in-Publication Data

Names: Denton, Michelle.
Title: Inclusion matters / Michelle Denton.
Description: Buffalo, NY : PowerKids Press, 2025. | Series: Disability pride | Includes glossary and index.
Identifiers: ISBN 9781499446777 (pbk.) | ISBN 9781499446784 (library bound) | ISBN 9781499446791 (ebook)
Subjects: LCSH: People with disabilities–Juvenile literature. | People with disabilities–Social conditions–Juvenile literature. | People with disabilities–Civil rights–Juvenile literature.
Classification: LCC HV1568.D476 2025 | DDC 362.4–dc23

Manufactured in the United States of America

Some of the images in this book illustrate individuals who are models. The depictions do not imply actual situations or events.

CPSIA Compliance Information: Batch #CSPK25. For Further Information contact Rosen Publishing at 1-800-237-9932.

Contents

Inclusion Is Important

Disabilities come in all shapes and sizes. Some affect the brain and are invisible to other people. Some affect the body and require the use of **equipment** such as wheelchairs, braces, or **prosthetic** arms and legs. People are sometimes born with a disability, and other times people become disabled because of an accident or illness.

Sometimes, just getting into a building or talking in a group can be more difficult for people with disabilities. They may need extra help. That's where inclusion comes in. When someone is included, they have the same **access** and opportunity to do things as everyone else.

The disability pride flag was created to show acceptance and respect for people who have disabilities. Each color is for a different type of disability.

- The gray background is in honor of those who've died.
- Green is for disabilities that have to do with the senses.
- Blue is for those that have to with the mind and emotions.
- White stands for unseen disabilities, as well as those that haven't been diagnosed, or found out.
- Gold is for neurodiversity.
- Red is for other disabilities of the body.

With some supportive equipment, such as this specialized wheelchair, people with disabilities can take part in games and sports.

In the Past

For people without disabilities, inclusion hasn't always been so important. Only 50 years ago, there were separate schools for children with disabilities. It was common for people with mental and physical disabilities to be put away in hospitals by their families. Society looked down on people with disabilities, and they were often treated badly.

It wasn't until 1971 that the **United Nations** (UN) announced that people with disabilities deserve the same rights and opportunities as everyone else. Then, in 1975, the Declaration on the Rights of Disabled Persons put these words into action and outlined the ways that governments around the world could help people with disabilities gain equality.

These photos show classrooms from the early 1900s and 1930s, where children with disabilities were separated from their peers in school.

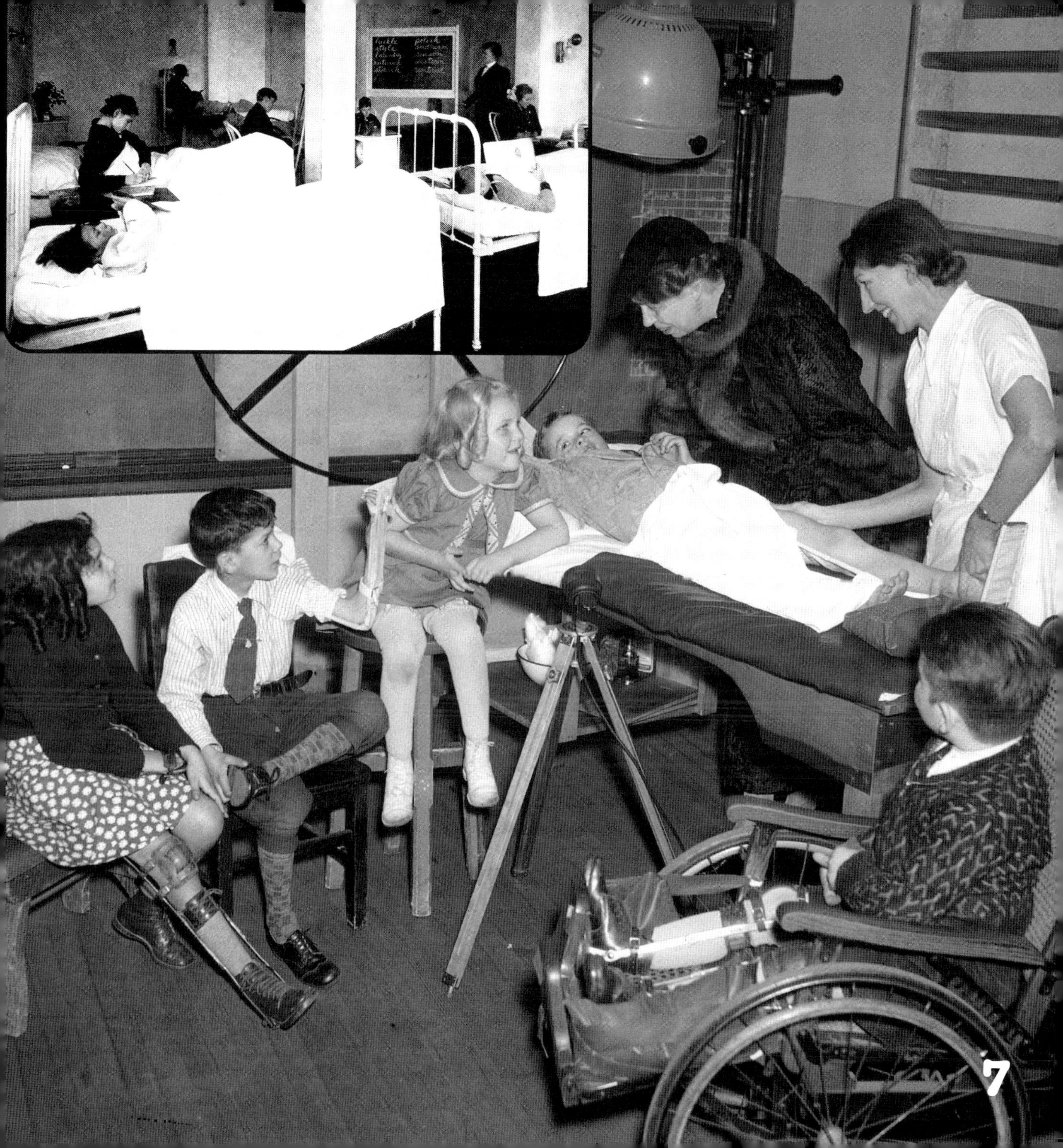

The United Nations' Action Plan

The UN continues to advocate, or speak up, for people with disabilities. The Disability Inclusion **Strategy** is a plan to actively involve people with disabilities in creating policies that will help them, as well as to create **benchmarks** to make sure that participating countries are progressing through the plan on time.

An important part of the strategy is its focus on **representation**. By hiring people with disabilities to make decisions that will affect other people with disabilities, the UN is letting the disability community speak for itself. This can also be seen in organizations like the American Association of People with Disabilities.

Lauren Potter (shown here) is an actress with Down syndrome. She and others like her are actively involved in making decisions and speaking up for the disability community.

Learn More

The United States passed the Americans with Disabilities Act (ADA) in 1990, setting many protections into law, such as banning job **discrimination** and ensuring access to public transportation and entry to public buildings.

In Schools and at Work

All students have the right to learn. This means that everyone in school should have the opportunity to gain as much knowledge as they can and reach their full **potential**. To help accomplish this goal, students with disabilities are allowed reasonable **accommodations** in the classroom, such as extra time on tests or having another student take notes for them. Textbooks can be provided in braille for blind students, and deaf students can be assigned to a teacher who knows sign language.

Learn More

The World Health Organization reports that as many as 240 million children worldwide live with disabilities. About half of those people have never attended school.

Disability accommodations are also found in the working world. Businesses are required to give workers the tools they need to succeed, including longer deadlines, more breaks, and special equipment.

Braille is a system of writing for the blind that uses characters made up of raised dots. Learning to read braille is something every blind person should have the opportunity to do.

Inclusive Design

Designing inclusively means creating things that are accessible to as many people as possible. How products and places are built affects who can interact with them. If the handle on a kitchen tool is too small or too smooth, a person with weak hands may not be able to grip it. If an office building only has stairs, a person on crutches may not be able to work there.

In the United States, the ADA sets standards for accessible building design. Entrances, restrooms, telephones, and drinking fountains are required to be accessible from a wheelchair, and signs must have braille on them for blind people.

Setting up wheelchair lifts is one way to make buildings more inclusive.

Learn More

Housing for individuals with mobility issues, or difficulty moving around, remains a large problem in the United States. Reports show that fewer than 1 in 100 homes are wheelchair accessible and fewer than 4 in 100 are accessible for people with moderate mobility difficulties.

Online and On-Screen

Even websites and advertisements are often inclusively designed. Word size and contrast matter a lot to people with visual disabilities, so marketing designers make sure that their messages can be seen by everyone. Other common online accessibility solutions are screen reader applications (apps) that read what's on a screen out loud.

Good representation is also important. This means that people with disabilities are shown on-screen or written about in realistic ways. For a long time, disabled characters in movies and books were often **stereotypes** or joked about unkindly. However, the disability rights movement has changed our culture by advocating for fair and respectful representation.

Gavin McHugh is a boy with cerebral palsy. He's also a famous actor! McHugh plays a young boy, Christopher, on the TV show *9-1-1*.

Community Inclusion

Accessibility and accommodations are two easy ways to include people with disabilities in a community. However, providing people with disabilities with a strong sense of community is just as important. Everyone can do this by being respectful and welcoming.

Many places are underused by people with disabilities because of a lack of knowledge about what services are available. Find out what kind of disability support services are provided at your favorite places and share that information with others.

Groups that include people with disabilities benefit from their unique, or one of a kind, strengths and ideas.

The language we use can also be a tool for inclusion. If you hear someone using unkind words to talk to or about people with disabilities, speak up or tell a trusted adult!

In the Future

As technology gets better, disability inclusion also gets better. By creating new ways people with disabilities can interact with other people and their environments, it becomes easier to provide access to places and activities. Some examples of technologies that help people with disabilities are hearing aids, voice assistants, **mechanical** lifts, and pill dispensers with timers.

However, the cost of aid devices can be very high. Hearing aids on average cost $2,000 each and last for five years. If you wore two hearing aids over 10 years, you would likely spend $8,000 or more, or about $67 a month.

Learn More

Prosthetic arms in the United States can cost anywhere from $5,000 for a simple prosthetic that only looks like an arm to $100,000 for a functional robotic prosthetic.

Prosthetic hands can type on keyboards and even use touchscreens.

Inclusion and You

Young people, both disabled and non-disabled, can support disability inclusion by joining clubs or sports that welcome people with disabilities, spreading the word about disability services at local places, and making sure that all people feel welcome.

Even with improvements to technology, there are limits. Many disabilities are permanent, something people will have their entire lives. It's likely that someone you know is disabled, even if you can't see it. Because of this we should respect other people's limits. If someone says they can't do something because of a disability, you should be respectful of their boundary.

All people deserve to feel like a valuable part of their community.

Learn More

Gatorland in Orlando, Florida, has opened the Gator Gauntlet, a new accessible ride that allows people in wheelchairs to travel down a zip line over the park and its lake of giant alligators.

Glossary

access: The ability to use or enter something.

accommodation: Something supplied that is useful and handy.

benchmark: A standard against which things are compared or assessed.

design: To create a plan for something.

discrimination: The treating of some people better than others without any fair or proper reason.

equipment: Supplies or tools needed for a certain purpose.

mechanical: Made or operated by a machine or machinery.

potential: Something that can develop or become real.

prosthetic: Of or relating to an artificial device that replaces a missing or injured part of the body.

representation: To present an individual as an example of the whole group.

stereotype: A commonly held idea about a group of people that isn't necessarily true.

strategy: A plan of action to achieve a goal.

United Nations (UN): An organization formed in 1945 to promote international cooperation.

For More Information

BOOKS

Evans, Nicole. *Disability Etiquette*. Ann Arbor, MI: Cherry Lake Press, 2023.

Mach, Jo Meserve, and Vera Lynne Stroup-Rentier. *Neema Wants to Learn: A True Story of Inclusion*. Topeka, KS: Find My Way Books, 2020.

Sanders, Jayneen. *Included: A Book for All Children About Inclusion, Diversity, Disability, Equality, and Empathy*. Victoria, Australia: Educate2Empower, 2022.

WEBSITES

Centers for Disease Control and Prevention (CDC): Kids' Quest
www.cdc.gov/ncbddd/kids/index.html
The CDC provides a selection of kid-centered articles about a number of different disabilities, each with their own list of online resources to learn more.

Job Accommodation Network
askjan.org/soar.cfm
A searchable database of accommodation recommendations for a variety of mental and physical disabilities.

Understood
www.understood.org
This nonprofit organization focuses on providing resources for people who learn and think differently, as well as for their caregivers and teachers.

Index